Dopefrica Presents

TRIVIA AFRICA

Quiz Book

Volume One

Questions & Answers about Africa

Dopefrica Publishing

www.dopefrica.com

About

Quiz Book

From the makers of the app Trivia Africa comes the first volume of the Trivia Africa Quiz Book. Containing over 100 questions in seven categories about the beautiful African continent, your knowledge of Africa will be tested.

CONTENTS

ARTS

Everything form African artwork to music, movies and the great people that create!

1 Which film was the first Netflix film produced in Nigeria?

2 What art form originates from West Africa and is highly characterised by the use of gold to reflect a great deal of value?

3 Which is Egypt's largest electronic music festival?

4 Which movie portrays the life of Mutesi, a Ugandan young girl who possesses an uncanny talent for chess?

5 What African music festival has its roots in Zanzibar?

6 Which Ghanaian is best known as the inventor of Afro-Jazz?

7 The Nyege Nyege Festival is held in the _____ of Africa

8 What music genre emerged in Zambia in the 1970s?

9 Nigerian cinema is known as _____

10 Which festival takes place in the week of Fela Kuti's birthday?

11 Which music festival takes place in Marrakech, Morocco?

12 Affectionately known as MaBrrr by her fans, this artist was described as the "Queen of African pop" and the "Madonna of the Townships".

13 Who released the album "African Giant" in 2019?

14 Which comedian made jokes about Oprah, Julius Malema and Jacob Zuma in his comedy special, Daywalker?

15 This Kenyan actress was awarded an Oscar for her role as Patsey in 12 years a slave.

16 What is the stage name for South African singer-songwriter Maya Christinah Xichavo Wegerif?

17 What 49m tall bronze statue is located in Dakar, Senegal commemorating Senegal's 50th independence anniversary from France?

18 What is the ancient Egyptian writing system called?

19 Which South African soap opera premiered in 1994 and once guest starred American artist, Chris Brown?

20 What animal is Timon from the Lion King?

Answers

1. Lionheart

2. Akan Art

3. Sandbox

4. Katwe

5. Sauti za Busara

6. Kofi Ghanaba

7. East

8. Zamrock

9. Nollywood

10. Felabration

11. Oasis Festival

12. Brenda Fassie

13. Burnaboy

14. Trevor Noah

15. Lupita Nyong'o

16. Sho Madjozi

17. African Renaissance Monument

18. Hieroglyphics

19. Generations

20. Yemi Alade

ECONOMY

Whether its currencies or industries, all the questions about Africa's economies.

1 What is Zambia's currency?

2 What does ECOWAS stand for?

3 What is Lesotho's currency?

4 True/False: Botswana belongs to ECOWAS.

5 What currency is used in Algeria?

6   What does SADC stand for?

7   What currency is Angola's currency?

8   What African country is the eighth largest oil exporter in the world?

9   What currency is used in Liberia?

10   What African country is the eighth largest oil exporter in the world?

11 What currency is used in Madagascar?

12 What is the area of Zambia where copper is mined called?

13 What currency is used in Mauritius?

14 What is Zimbabwe's principal agricultural export?

15 What currency is used in Sierra Leone?

16 What does COMESA stand for?

17 What is Botswana's currency?

18 True/False: The continent has the largest reserves of precious metals

19 What currency is used in Djibouti?

20 Which country is often referred to as the 'Giant of Africa', owing to its large population and economy?

ECONOMY
Answers

1. Kwacha

2. Economic Community of West African States

3. Loti

4. False

5. Dinar

6. Southern African Development Community

7. Kwanza

8. Nigeria

9. Copperbelt

10. Nigeria

11. Ariary

12. Copperbelt

13. Mauritian Rupee

14. Tobacco

15. Leonne

16. Common Market for Eastern and Southern Africa

17. Pula

18. True

19. Franc

20. Nigeria

GEOGRAPHY

Most people know Africa's geography more than anything else, but how well do you really know it?

1 Which African country is the only one in the world to lie entirely one thousand metres above sea level?

2 Timbuktu is in which country?

3 Which city is located at the confluence of the White Nile and the Blue Nile?

4 Name the principal river of western Africa?

5 Today, the term Greater Maghreb corresponds roughly to which 16th to 19th century region?

6 Kano and Lagos are two large cities in which country?

 7 One of the oldest university in the world is found in...

 8 Which is Africa's largest lake?

 9 The capital city of Uganda is

_____

 **10** Burkina Faso's capital is

_____

11 Freetown is the capital city for

_____

12 Which country hosted the 2010 FIFA World Cup?

13 Which ocean/sea encompasses Africa to the east?

14 What is the capital city of Namibia?

15 The Vaal river can be found in

_____

16
Which country's capital is Porto-Novo?

17
Which country formerly known as the Republic of Volta was renamed by then-President Thomas Sankara in 1984?

18
What island, off the coast of Mauritania/Senegal, has Portuguese as its official language?

19
What country's capital is called Yaounde?

20
N'Djamena is the largest city in

_____

GEOGRAPHY Answers

1. Lesotho

2. Mali

3. Khartoum

4. Niger

5. Morocco

6. Nigeria

7. Mali

8. Lake Victoria

9. Kampala

10. Ouagadougou

11. Sierra Leone

12. South Africa

13. Indian Ocean

14. Windhoek

15. South Africa

16. Benin

17. Burkina Faso

18. Cape Verde

19. Cameroon

20. Chad

HISTORY

The past should not be easily forgotten because it is the foundation, how much do you know about Africa's history?

1 The Democratic Republic of the Congo became independent from which country in 1960?

2 Who was Ethiopia's regent from 1916 to 1930, and Emperor from 1930 to 1974?

3 Who was a renowned Kenyan social, environmental and political activist and the first African woman to win the Nobel Prize?

4 In 1990, he was released from prison to become the first black president of the Republic of South Africa.

5 As one of South Africa's human rights activists, he won the1984 Nobel Peace Prize for his efforts in resolving and ending apartheid.

 **6** He led Tanzania as president from 1964 to 1985 following his tenure as prime minister of Tanganyika...

 7 Who assumed the Rwandan presidency in 22 April 2000?

 **8** In 1960, he visited Martin Luther King Jr & afterwards, in July 1961, organised a civil disobedience campaign in Northern Province of Zambia.

 9 He led his country as its first president in 1964 to his death in 1978. He has an international airport named after him in Nairobi.

 **10** Who reigned as King of the Zulu kingdom from 1816 and ended by his assassination in 1828?

11 Which year did Libya get independence from British & French oversight?

12 Benin, Niger, Chad and Gabon all gained independence in which month?

13 At its peak, this was one of the largest states in African history that dominated the western Sahel in the 15th and 16th century.

14 What was the name given to the Australopithecus fossil discovered in Ethiopia?

15 In what year was the Organisation of African Unity(OAU) formed?

16 In what year did Togo gain independence?

17 When did Zimbabwe gain its independence from British colonisation?

18 What has been regarded as the shortest war in recorded history?

19 Apartheid was a form of government that was present in _____ up until 1994.

20 In what year was Nelson Mandela released from prison after 27 years?

HISTORY Answers

1. Belgium

2. Haile Selassie

3. Wangari Maathai

4. Nelson Mandela

5. Desmond Tutu

6. Julius Nyerere

7. Paul Kagame

8. Kenneth Kaunda

9. Jomo Kenyatta

10. Shaka

11. 1951

12. August

13. Songhai

14. Lucy

15. 1963

16. 1960

17. 1980

18. Anglo-Zanzibar War

19. South Africa

20. 1990

NATURE

Questions from Kilimanjaro, the Nile to elephants and lions.

1 What colour best describes a giraffe's tongue?

2 What large land animal kills the most people in Africa?

3 Name the principal river of western Africa?

4 Which is Africa's largest lake?

5 What large southern African lake takes its name from the country in which it can be found?

 **6** At about 4100 miles, this is the longest river in the world.

 7 The highest peak of Mt Kilimanjaro is called _____

 8 How fast can an ostrich sprint?

 9 What habitat covers 25% of Africa and is mainly found in the north?

 **10** This is a river southwest of Africa that originates in Angola and ends in a delta in Botswana.

11 What is the fastest that the cheetah run?

12 Which country is best known as the former home of the now extinct bird, the dodo?

13 What does the term "Mosi oa tunya" mean?

14 What southern African former lake is now considered one of the largest salt pans in the world?

15 A lion's roar can be heard up to a distance of _____

16 Which tree native to Africa is known as "The Tree of Life" because it provides shelter, water and food?

17 Which animal is best known for its "laughing" call?

18 What river supplies the Victoria Falls?

19 What is the national bird of Zambia?

20 What is Benin's national animal?

NATURE
Answers

1. Blue

2. Hippopotamus

3. Niger

4. Lake Victoria

5. Lake Malawi

6. The Nile

7. Kibo

8. 43mph

9. Desert

10. Okavango River

11. 120mph

12. Mauritius

13. Smoke that thunders

14. Makgadikgadi

15. 5 miles

16. Baobab

17. Hyena

18. Zambezi River

19. African Fish Eagle

20. Leopard

PEOPLE

Questions about remarkable & interesting Africans change Africa and the world.

1 Which ethnic group inhabiting northern Tanzania and southern Kenya is the stretching of earlobes a common practice?

2 Kofi Annan, the seventh Secretary-General of the United Nations from 1997 to 2006, was what nationality?

3 This novelist from Nigeria is famed for writing "Things Fall Apart" in 1958.

4 In 1990, he was released from prison to become the first black president of the Republic of South Africa.

5 He led Tanzania as president from 1964 to 1985 following his tenure as prime minister of Tanganyika...

6 Davido is best known for which African music genre?

 7 He led his country as its first president in 1964 to his death in 1978. He has an international airport named after him in Nairobi.

 8 She is a world-renowned Somali-American model with an illustruous career and a cosmetics business.

9 Nicknamed as Mama Africa, she was a South African singer, songwriter, actress, United Nations goodwill ambassador & civil rights activist ca.

 **10** Who sang the song "Umqombothi" which was featured in the opening scene of the 2004 movie Hotel Rwanda?

36

11 Who has served as minister of Education in Uganda since June 2016?

12 The winner of the 2019 Miss Universe is from _____

13 Where is musician-turned-politician, Bobi Wine, from?

14 On 12 August 2008, Benjamin Boukpeti won a bronze medal in the Men's K1 Kayak Slalom at the Olympics. Which country did he compete for?

15 Who was "so good that they had to name him twice"?

16 This Ugandan-British artist attended the University of Cambridge and has an award winning podcast on the BBC.

17 Which American celebrity was granted Gabonese citizenship in 2019?

18 Who is the president of Cape Verde or Cabo Verde (as of 2022)?

19 Who succeeded Mwai Kibaki as president of Kenya?

20 Who was the first ethnically black player to play for the South African national cricket team?

PEOPLE
Answers

1. The Maasai

2. Ghanian

3. Chinua Achebe

4. Nelson Mandela

5. Julius Nyerere

6. Afrobeats

7. Jomo Kenyatta

8. Iman Abdulmajid

9. Miriam Makeba

10. Yvonne Chaka Chaka

11. Janet Museveni

12. South Africa

13. Uganda

14. Togo

15. Jay Jay Okocha

16. George the poet

17. Chris "Ludacris" Bridges

18. José Maria Neves

19. Uhuru Kenyatta

20. Makhaya Ntini

SPORT

These questions cover more than just football and long distance running (we promise).

1 What does AFCON stand for?

2 Which country won the 2012 AFCON?

3 Which country hosted the 2010 FIFA World Cup?

4 What name, literally translated as 'the boys, the boys' is the nickname for South Africa's men's national football team?

5 The Nigerian football team is also known as the _____

 **6** What sport, other than football, is popular in South Africa, Zimbabwe, Morocco, Namibia and Ivory Coast?

 7 Which country tops the olympics medals table for African countries?

 8 Who won the gold medal at the 2012 Summer Olympics, giving her country (Tunisia) its first Olympic medal by a woman?

 9 What was the 2010 World Cup football called?

 **10** Which country won the 2019 Rugby World Cup?

11 Which Cameroonian footballer won the African Player of the Years in 2003, 2004, 2005, and 2010?

12 Who facilitated a cease fire in his country after 5 years of civil war when the national team qualified for the 2006 FA World Cup?

13 Who won the 2013 Berlin Marathon and beat the world record in 2h 3mins 23sec?

14 Who is the first black South African rugby captain who led the springboks to victory in the 2019 world cup?

15 Where was the 2012 African Cup of Nations held?

16 The Eagles of Carthage is the football team name of which north African country?

17 What is the South African rugby team commonly known as?

18 Which South African played for Leeds United and was nicknamed "Rhoo"?

19 What movie was based on John Carlin's Book "Playing the Enemy: Nelson Mandela and the Game that Made a Nation"?

20 Which Mozambican athlete specialised in the 800m and is a three-time world champion?

SPORT Answers

1. Africa Cup of Nations

2. Zambia

3. South Africa

4. Bafana Bafana

5. Super Eagles

6. Rugby

7. Kenya

8. Habiba Ghribi

9. Jabulani

10. South Africa

11. Samuel E'to

12. Didier Drogba

13. Wilson Kipsang Kiprotich

14. Siya Kolisi

15. Gabon

16. Tunisia

17. Springboks

18. Lucas Radebe

19. Invictus

20. Maria Mutola

For more questions, make sure to download the Trivia Africa app

 For more information visit
www.dopefrica.com

Trivia Africa
Features:

CLASSIC MODE

60 seconds to answer as many questions from our database of hundreds of multiple-choice questions and set a high score!

For more information visit
www.dopefrica.com

Trivia Africa
Features:

TRUE/FALSE MODE

The answer is the flip of a coin but you only have 60 seconds to answer as many questions as possible.

For more information visit
www.dopefrica.com

Trivia Africa
Features:

FLAG QUIZ MODE

Match the flag with its country. Can you match all 54 flags to their countries?

 For more information visit
www.dopefrica.com

Trivia Africa
Features:

FUNDA MODE

Funda (pronounced "foon duh") is the Zulu word for "Learn". Learn about Africa with this fun mode!

 For more information visit
www.dopefrica.com

Trivia Africa
Features:

10 QUESTIONS MODE

10 questions & 10 seconds per question.

 *For more information visit*
www.dopefrica.com

Trivia Africa
Features:

STREAK MODE

Correctly answer as many questions as possible in a roll.

For more information visit
www.dopefrica.com

Trivia Africa
Features:

LEADERBOARD

Log in with your Google or Facebook (or Apple on iOS) accounts to post your best scores to our global Trivia Africa Leaderboard.

 For more information visit
www.dopefrica.com

Play with against a friend or in teams:

 For more information visit
www.dopefrica.com

NOTES

www.dopefrica.com.

www.dopefrica.com.

www.dopefrica.com.

www.dopefrica.com.

Printed in Great Britain
by Amazon